A REASON FOR WRITING

"WORDS OF WISDOM"

This book belongs to:

A Concerned Communications Publication

authors: Carol Ann Retzer and Eva Hoshino
senior editor: Bill Morelan
copy editor: Patricia Horning Benton
cover design: Daniel Potter
cover and inside illustrations: Mary Bausman
inside design: Walt Woesner
Scripture border sheets: Rita Hoshino and Sarah Thurstenson

For more information about A REASON FOR WRITING®, write or call:
Concerned Communications
P.O. Box 1000
Siloam Springs, Arkansas 72761
Telephone (501) 549-9000

Printed in U.S.A.

To be consistent with the traditional form in reference to God, pronouns referring to God are capitalized.

Printed on recycled paper

Grab your skates, it's time to write!

Handwriting is like learning to ride a skate board or roller blades. They are all motor skills. And any motor skill takes practice.

Do you remember the first time you got on a skate board or tried roller blading? Once you got going were you sure you could stop? By now you are probably a pro. But that didn't happen the first day or maybe not even the first week, or first month. It took plenty of practice.

Mastering cursive writing is like learning any motor skill. It takes a lot of practice. The more you practice, the better your writing looks and the more legible it is. Handwriting is an important life skill. While we may each have a unique writing skill, the basics of letter formation are important to aid in the ease and legibility of writing.

Actually 25% of spelling errors are not because people don't know how to spell the words, but because they weren't careful in making letters a, e, i, o, and u. Especially notice how you form these letters.

The lessons in this book are designed to share with you some basic life skills as well as handwriting skills. These verse lessons from Proverbs contain words of wisdom for a happy life. The words and letters you practice will sharpen your writing skills.

Hopefully you'll be able to share the verses you have written on a border sheet with others. Many people have told us how it brightened their life to receive a verse from a student. In fact, some have said that the verse arrived at just the time they needed it. Perhaps you can be God's messenger as you share His word through a verse lesson.

Now have fun skate boarding, roller blading - and writing!

Proper Hand and Paper Position

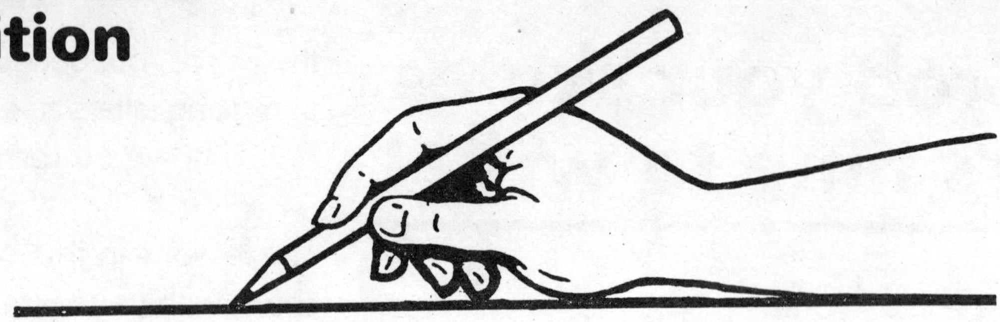

Right-handed

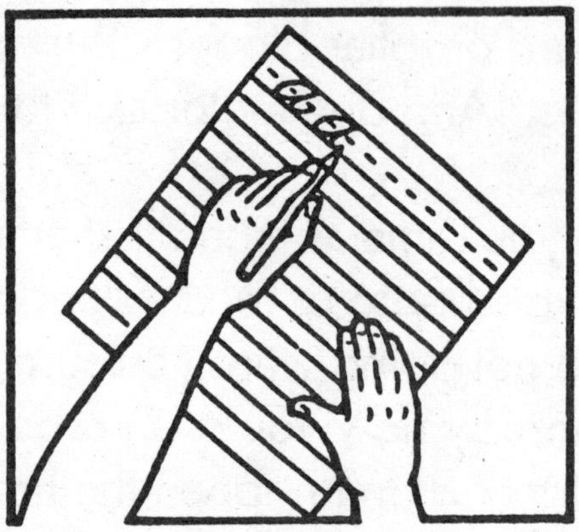

Left-handed

Correct Cursive Formation of Letters and Numbers

A B C D E F G H I J K L M

N O P Q R S T U V W X Y Z

a b c d e f g h i j k l m n

o p q r s t u v w x y z

1 2 3 4 5 6 7 8 9 10

Self-Check Hints for Better Handwriting

Have you ever thought about how your teacher grades your handwriting? She probably keeps several things in mind when she looks at your paper. Why not beat her to the job!

Look at a page of your handwriting. Then see how your paper measures up in these areas:

✍ **Formation:** Is each letter formed correctly, without extra tails and curls? Check the chart if you can't remember how to make a letter.

✍ **Spacing:** Is the spacing even between letters? Is there enough space between words?

✍ **Slant:** Do the letters slant forward without falling over? The slant should be consistent on the whole page.

✍ **Capitals:** Is each capital a full space tall? Does each sentence begin with a capital letter? Are all proper names and pronouns referring to God also capitalized?

✍ **Punctuation:** Does each sentence end with the correct punctuation mark? Are other punctuation marks, such as apostrophes and quotation marks, included where necessary?

✍ **Numbers:** Does each number come only to the dotted line?

What kind of a grade do you give your own handwriting? Easy-to-read handwriting is a skill you'll need your whole life, so keep working!

Weekly Schedule

Day 1

Read the handwriting tip at the first of the lesson. Then carefully practice the letters and words for the day.

Day 2

You'll have new letters and words from the Verse of the Week to practice today in this book.

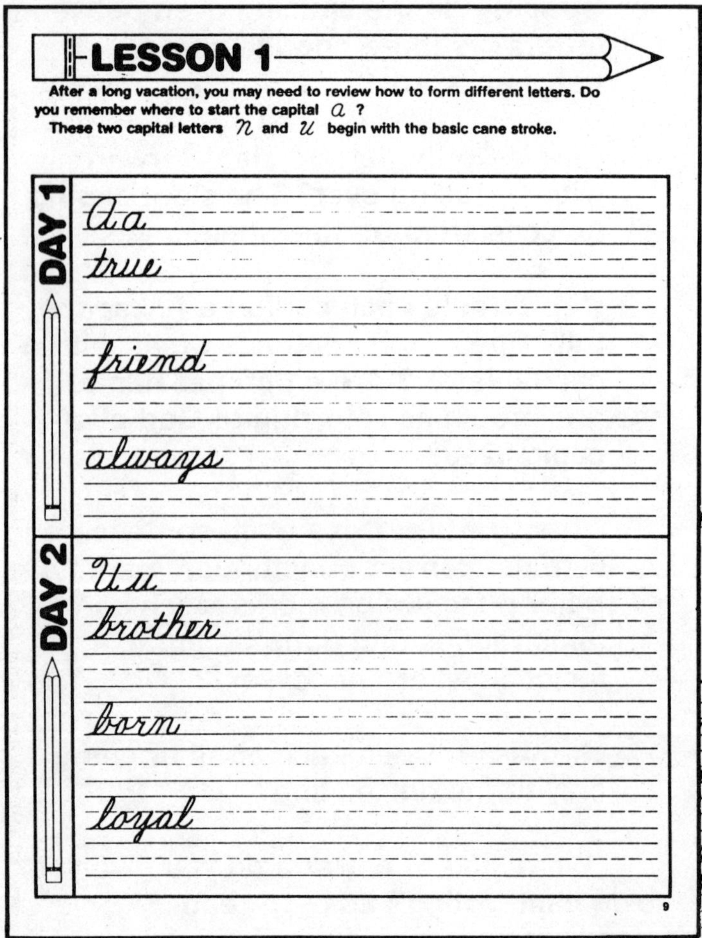

LESSON 1

After a long vacation, you may need to review how to form different letters. Do you remember where to start the capital *a* ?
These two capital letters *n* and *u* begin with the basic cane stroke.

DAY 1

Aa
true
friend
always

DAY 2

Uu
brother
born
loyal

9

Day 3

Review the handwriting tip. Make sure you're forming letters and words correctly as you practice. After you've finished practicing, take a moment to look back over the whole lesson to see how your handwriting measures up against the model.

Day 4

Write the verse on practice paper at least once. If you have time, start coloring the Scripture border sheet you'll finish tomorrow.

Day 5

In your best handwriting, write the Verse of the Week on your Scripture border sheet. Finish decorating the border. Think of someone who would enjoy your beautiful verse. Smile as you give it to that person.

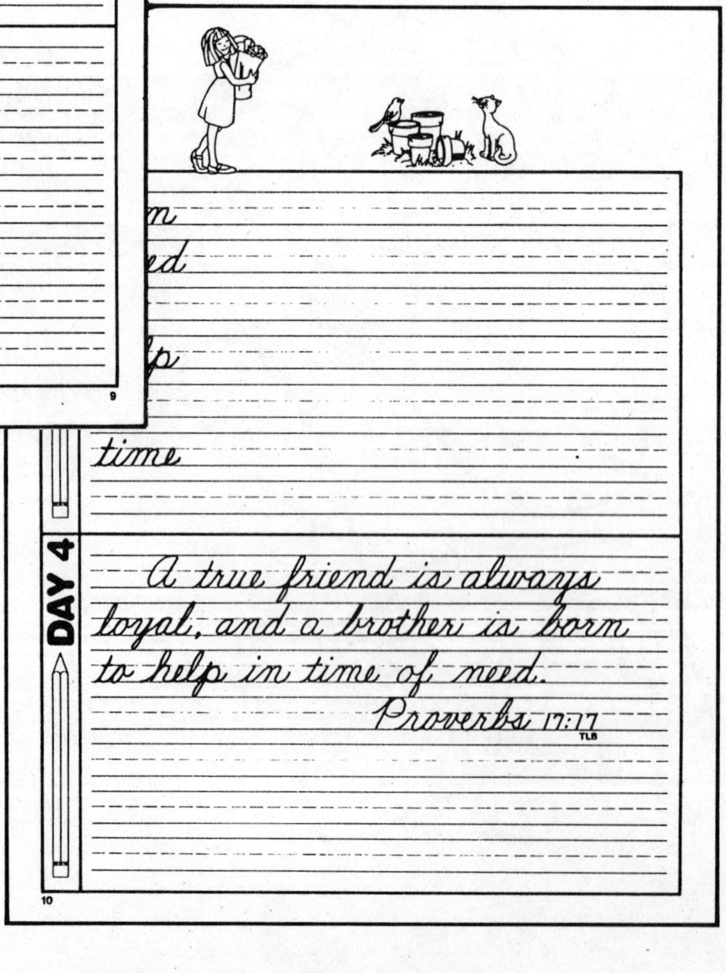

n
ed
p
time

DAY 4

A true friend is always loyal, and a brother is born to help in time of need.
Proverbs 17:17 TLB

10

WEEKLY LESSONS

CURSIVE

A Reason For Writing

LESSON 1

After a long vacation, you may need to review how to form different letters. Do you remember where to start the capital *A* ?

These two capital letters *N* and *U* begin with the basic cane stroke.

DAY 1

Aa

true

friend

always

DAY 2

Uu

brother

born

loyal

DAY 3

Nn

need

help

time

DAY 4

A true friend is always
loyal, and a brother is born
to help in time of need.

Proverbs 17:17 TLB

LESSON 2

The capitals *D* and *O* begin at the 2 o'clock position. Make each with a counterclockwise stroke.

Do you want to be successful? The verse this week can help you have a good school year!

DAY 1

Dd

Despise

Word

find

DAY 2

Gg

God's

yourself

trouble

DAY 3

W

Obey

and

succeed

DAY 4

Despise God's Word
and find yourself in trouble.
Obey it and succeed.

Proverbs 13:13
TLB

LESSON 3

Be sure to use a *question mark* (?) at the end of the question.

Here's a question for you to think about. What does it mean to *reverence* the Lord?

DAY 1

How

does

man

become

DAY 2

The

wise

first

step

DAY 3

Lord

trust

reverence

and

DAY 4

How does a man become wise? The first step is to trust and reverence the Lord!

Proverbs 1:7 TLB

LESSON 4

It's important to connect letters so they can be read easily. Watch these combinations this week: *ch* and *ct* .

What do your actions tell other people about you? Can they see that you are a Christian?

DAY 1

Cc

child

The

character

DAY 2

Ee

even

known

acts

DAY 3

Rr

right

whether

pure

DAY 4

The character of even a child can be known by the way he acts—whether what he does is pure and right.

Proverbs 20:11 TLB

LESSON 5

These two capital letters *J* and *K* are not joined to the letter that follows.

Have you ever been disciplined by your dad? Did you know that he loved you even through the punishment?

DAY 1

Jj

Just

father

punishes

DAY 2

son

delights

make

better

DAY 3

L

Lord

corrects

you

DAY 4

Just as a father punishes
a son he delights in to
make him better, so the
Lord corrects you.

Proverbs 3:12 TLB

LESSON 6

This week you'll practice three capital letters that begin in different places:

- The *I* begins at the bottom right.
- The *O* begins at 2 o'clock.
- The *Q* begins with a top loop.

DAY 1

Ii

It

honor

man

DAY 2

Oo

Only

stay

fight

DAY 3

Qq

quarreling

fools

insist

DAY 4

It is an honor for a man to stay out of a fight. Only fools insist on quarreling.

Proverbs 20:3 TLB

LESSON 7

Do a page check this week. Are all the letters slanted the same way and the same amount? Work on making your slant easy to read.

Think about the verse for this week. Should Christian kids be understanding with their teachers and parents?

DAY 1

F

For

reverence

fear

DAY 2

God

basic

wisdom

results

DAY 3

Cc

Knowing

kind

understanding

DAY 4

For the reverence and fear of God are basic to all wisdom. Knowing God results in every other kind of understanding.

Proverbs 9:10 TLB

LESSON 8

Look at the baseline. Are all your letters sitting where they belong? Which letters should go below the baseline?

Had you ever thought of a lie as a deadly weapon? This verse says a lie can hurt as much as being hit with a weapon.

DAY 1

Tt

Telling

lies

someone

DAY 2

Xx

axe

harmful

wounding

DAY 3

Ss

sword

shooting

sharp

DAY 4

Telling lies about someone is as harmful as hitting him with an axe, or wounding him with a sword, or shooting him with a sharp arrow.

Proverbs 25:18 TLB

LESSON 9

Your name is the most important thing you write. Write it with care. Be proud of how good it looks on every paper you turn in this week.

DAY 1

I

It

better

hands

DAY 2

get

dirty

than

too

DAY 3

Vv

proud

work

starve

DAY 4

It is better to get your
hands dirty—and eat, than
to be too proud to work—
and starve.

Proverbs 12:9
TLB

LESSON 10

Ants at work are really fun to watch! They're always busy. See if you can work as hard this week as you practice your handwriting.

Be especially careful with your *T* 's, *L* 's, and *Z* 's.

DAY 1

T

Take

lesson

ants

DAY 2

L

Learn

lazy

fellow

DAY 3

Zz

from

ways

wise

DAY 4

Take a lesson from the ants, you lazy fellow. Learn from their ways and be wise!

Proverbs 6:6
TLB

LESSON 11

The verse this week can give you a lot to think about. What does it mean to be *persuasive*?

Why are kind words sweet like honey? Think for a moment about something kind that's been said to you. How did that make you feel?

DAY 1

F

From

wise

careful

DAY 2

mind

persuasive

speech

honey

DAY 3

K

Kind

enjoyable

healthful

DAY 4

From a wise mind comes careful and persuasive speech. Kind words are like honey—enjoyable and healthful.

Proverbs 16:23, 24
TLB

LESSON 12

Is your slant even? Here's a way to check.

Draw dotted lines through the down strokes, like the example. *when*

If you're writing carefully, these lines will be parallel and slanted the same. How does your page look?

DAY 1

Y

Your

own

soul

DAY 2

is

nourished

when

kind

DAY 3

it

destroyed

when

cruel

DAY 4

Your own soul is nourished when you are kind; it is destroyed when you are cruel.

Proverbs 11:17

TLB

LESSON 13

Notice the difference between *w* and *u*. Practice these difficult combinations this week: *we*, *wr*, *wo*, *ua*, *ur*, and *us*. By the end of the week you should have them mastered.

DAY 1

a

soft

answer

wrath

DAY 2

G

Gentle

harsh

quarrels

DAY 3

Zq

life

griping

discouragement

DAY 4

A soft answer turns away wrath, but harsh words cause quarrels. Gentle words cause life and health; griping brings discouragement.

Proverbs 15:1, 4 TLB

LESSON 14

Watch the lowercase letters and stay within the lines. Check to see whether your numbers are only as tall as the middle dotted line.

Are you enjoying these verses from Proverbs? Can you see why King Solomon is said to have been the wisest man who ever lived?

DAY 1

E

Everyone

enjoys

giving

DAY 2

J j

good

advice

wonderful

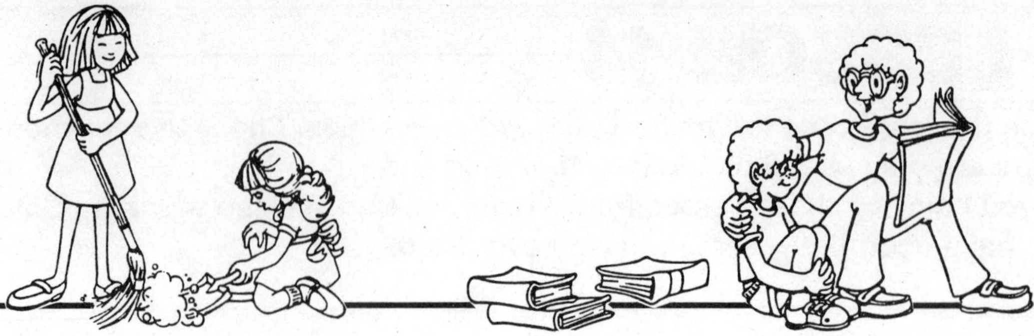

DAY 3

able

right

thing

time

DAY 4

Everyone enjoys giving
good advice, and how
wonderful it is to be able
to say the right thing at
the right time!

Proverbs 15:23
TLB

LESSON 15

Be sure to start each letter in the right place. See where the capital *I* starts. It's more efficient to write right (and besides, it's correct!).

Have you ever wanted to be an army officer? This verse says it's better to have self-control.

DAY 1

I

It

better

slow

DAY 2

be

tempered

famous

self

DAY 3

have

control

than

army

DAY 4

It is better to be slow-
tempered than famous; it
is better to have self-control
than to control an army.

Proverbs 16:32
TLB

LESSON 16

It's fun to make an exclamation mark! And it's fun to praise the Lord for the beautiful things He has made just for us!

DAY 1

W

When

gloomy

everything

DAY 2

is

man

wrong

cheerful

DAY 3

he

everything

seems

right

DAY 4

When a man is gloomy,
everything seems to go
wrong; when he is cheerful,
everything seems right!

Proverbs 15:15
TLB

LESSON 17

There's one shorter letter in the crowd. The *d*, *l*, *b*, *k*, and *h* all go clear to the top line. The "shorty" is the *t*, which stops halfway between the dotted line and the top line.

DAY 1

Bb

Be

patient

finally

DAY 2

Cc

you

soft

tongue

DAY 3

Rr

break

hard

bones

DAY 4

Be patient and you will finally win, for a soft tongue can break hard bones.

Proverbs 25:15 TLB

LESSON 18

To write faster, dot the *i* 's and cross the *t* 's *after* you've written the whole word.

And save yourself trouble by guarding your tongue! Can you find another verse in the Bible that talks about the tongue?

DAY 1

D

Don't

talk

much

DAY 2

You

keep

putting

foot

DAY 3

Be

sensible

turn

flow

DAY 4

Don't talk so much. You keep putting your foot in your mouth. Be sensible and turn off the flow!

Proverbs 10:19 TLB

LESSON 19

Why is this week's verse especially good to remember?

King Solomon's books are filled with special promises. If you want to become wise, pay attention to his words.

DAY 1

T

Telling

truth

gives

DAY 2

man

great

satisfaction

work

DAY 3

him

returns

many

blessings

DAY 4

Telling the truth gives a man great satisfaction, and hard work returns many blessings to him.

Proverbs 12:14 TLB

LESSON 20

It's time for another page check of your writing. If parts of letters are spaced unevenly, your page will look lopsided. Correctly formed letters make a uniform and easy-to-read sheet.

You're learning to improve your handwriting. How can you also write virtues deep within your heart?

DAY 1

N

Never

forget

truthful

DAY 2

H

Hold

kind

virtues

DAY 3

W

Write

tightly

within

DAY 4

Never forget to be truthful and kind. Hold these virtues tightly. Write them deep within your heart.

Proverbs 3:3 TLB

LESSON 21

To qualify as a quick student, answer this quiz question. In English, what pair of letters almost always go together? Can you find them in this lesson?

This question is not so easy. Why is it often so hard to stop a quarrel?

DAY 1

Ii

It

hard

stop

DAY 2

Qq

quarrel

starts

don't

DAY 3

Oo

once

let

begin

DAY 4

It is hard to stop a quarrel once it starts, so don't let it begin.

Proverbs 17:14 TLB

LESSON 22

The letters and words on each page are your models. Practice writing them carefully.

Watch these tough combinations: *er*, *ar*, *ir*, and *ro*.

DAY 1

Aa

Uu

cheerful

heart

DAY 2

Mm

medicine

does

good

DAY 3

but

broken

spirit

sick

DAY 4

A cheerful heart does good like medicine, but a broken spirit makes one sick.

Proverbs 17:22 TLB

LESSON 23

There are very few verses with a *Z* in them. But just the same, practice making this capital letter.

Remember that the lowercase *t* is *not* a loop letter. Keep the stem closed. Cross the *t* after you've finished the whole word.

DAY 1

Vv

favor

If

want

DAY 2

Zz

reputation

judgment

common

DAY 3

Lord

sense

trust

completely

DAY 4

If you want favor with both God and man, and a reputation for good judgment and common sense, then trust the Lord completely; don't ever trust yourself.

Proverbs 3:4,5 TLB

LESSON 24

Twins who look alike are fun! This week you can practice two vowel twins— *oo* and *ee*. Connecting these twins to other letters is a bit tricky.

What does Solomon mean by the term *a good name*? How much is a good name worth?

DAY 1

If

must

choose

good

DAY 2

name

rather

great

riches

DAY 3

gold

loving

esteem

silver

DAY 4

If you must choose, take
a good name rather than
great riches; for to be held
in loving esteem is better
than silver and gold.

Proverbs 22:1
TLB

LESSON 25

What does it mean to *reflect* something? Look in a mirror, then see if you can answer the question.

Think about your friends. What kind of a person do they show you to be?

DAY 1

Aa

mirror

reflects

face

DAY 2

Bb

but

what

really

DAY 3

Ss

shown

friends

chooses

DAY 4

A mirror reflects a man's face, but what he is really like is shown by the kind of friends he chooses.

Proverbs 27:19
TLB

LESSON 26

Work hard on *e* combinations this week, such as *ee*, *fe*, *se*, and *ea*.
Look at the three parts of the capital *W*. Are they the same height?

DAY 1

W

Wisdom

tree

life

DAY 2

eat

those

fruit

happy

DAY 3

who

keeps

man

eating

DAY 4

Wisdom is a tree of life
to those who eat her fruit;
happy is the man who
keeps on eating it.

Proverbs 3:18
TLB

LESSON 27

Don't forget to use an *apostrophe* (') when you put two words together. You'll notice that the apostrophe goes just below the middle dotted line.

DAY 1

D

Don't

conceited

wisdom

DAY 2

sure

Instead

trust

reverence

DAY 3

turn

Lord

back

evil

DAY 4

Don't be conceited, sure of your own wisdom. Instead, trust and reverence the Lord, and turn your back on evil.

Proverbs 3:7,8 TLB

LESSON 28

Remember that *j*, *f*, *y*, and *p* each has a part that goes below the baseline.

Make sure that your *o*'s end in an upswing and don't go down to the line and look like *a*'s.

DAY 1

We

justify

Ee

every

DAY 2

God

looks

motives

more

DAY 3

Mm

pleased

Him

gifts

DAY 4

We can justify our every deed but God looks at our motives. God is more pleased when we are just and fair than when we give Him gifts.

Proverbs 21:2, 3 TLB

LESSON 29

More twins in this lesson— *ll*, *ee*, and *ss*. Make them carefully.
Think about the things you love best. What would you guard most carefully?

DAY 1

F

Follow

My

advice

DAY 2

O

Obey

keep

stick

DAY 3

Me

Guard

precious

possession

DAY 4

Follow My advice ...; always keep it in mind and stick to it. Obey Me and live! Guard My words as your most precious possession.

Proverbs 7:1,2
TLB

LESSON 30

This week practice two letters that are *not* twins— *h* and *k* . On this page you can see that they are relatives—but not twins!

Have you ever been in trouble because you got off the main track? King Solomon warns Christians to stick to the path and be safe. That's good advice.

DAY 1

W

Watch

step

path

DAY 2

S

Stick

safe

pull

DAY 3

D

Don't

sidetrack

danger

DAY 4

Watch your step. Stick to the path and be safe. Don't sidetrack; pull back your foot from danger.

Proverbs 4:26, 27 TLB

LESSON 31

Round tops are what you want on your *n*'s and *m*'s. Be sure you know which has two humps and which three.

Keep the round motion going on these letters— *a*, *o*, *g*, *d*, and *c*.

DAY 1

I

would

learn

great

DAY 2

fact

wisest

life

kind

DAY 3

If

limp

stumble

run

DAY 4

I would have you learn this great fact: that a life of doing right is the wisest life there is. If you live that kind of life, you'll not limp or stumble as you run.

Proverbs 4:11, 12
TLB

LESSON 32

Make sure that your lowercase letters stay within the boundary lines. Be sure you dot your lowercase *i*'s and cross your *t*'s *after* you complete writing the word.

DAY 1

Ww

When

man

trying

DAY 2

G

God

please

worst

DAY 3

his

even

enemies

peace

DAY 4

When a man is trying to please God, God makes even his worst enemies to be at peace with him.

Proverbs 16:7 TLB

LESSON 33

Don't forget the upward curve stroke at the beginning of the lowercase *y*.
Watch how you write your *y*'s in *away*, *they*, *you*, and *energy*.
Are you working toward the twin goals of wisdom and common sense?

DAY 1

Have

two

goals

wisdom

DAY 2

sense

right

common

away

DAY 3

Don't

slip

energy

feather

DAY 4

Have two goals: wisdom—that is, knowing and doing right—and common sense. Don't let them slip away, for they fill you with living energy, and are a feather in your cap.

Proverbs 3:21, 22
TLB

BORDER SHEETS

CURSIVE

A Reason For Writing

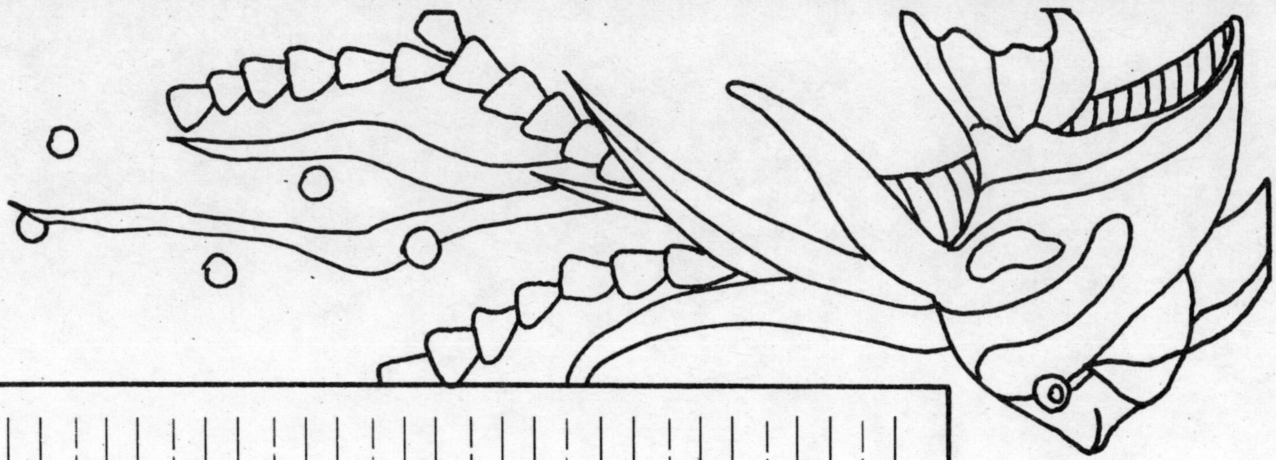

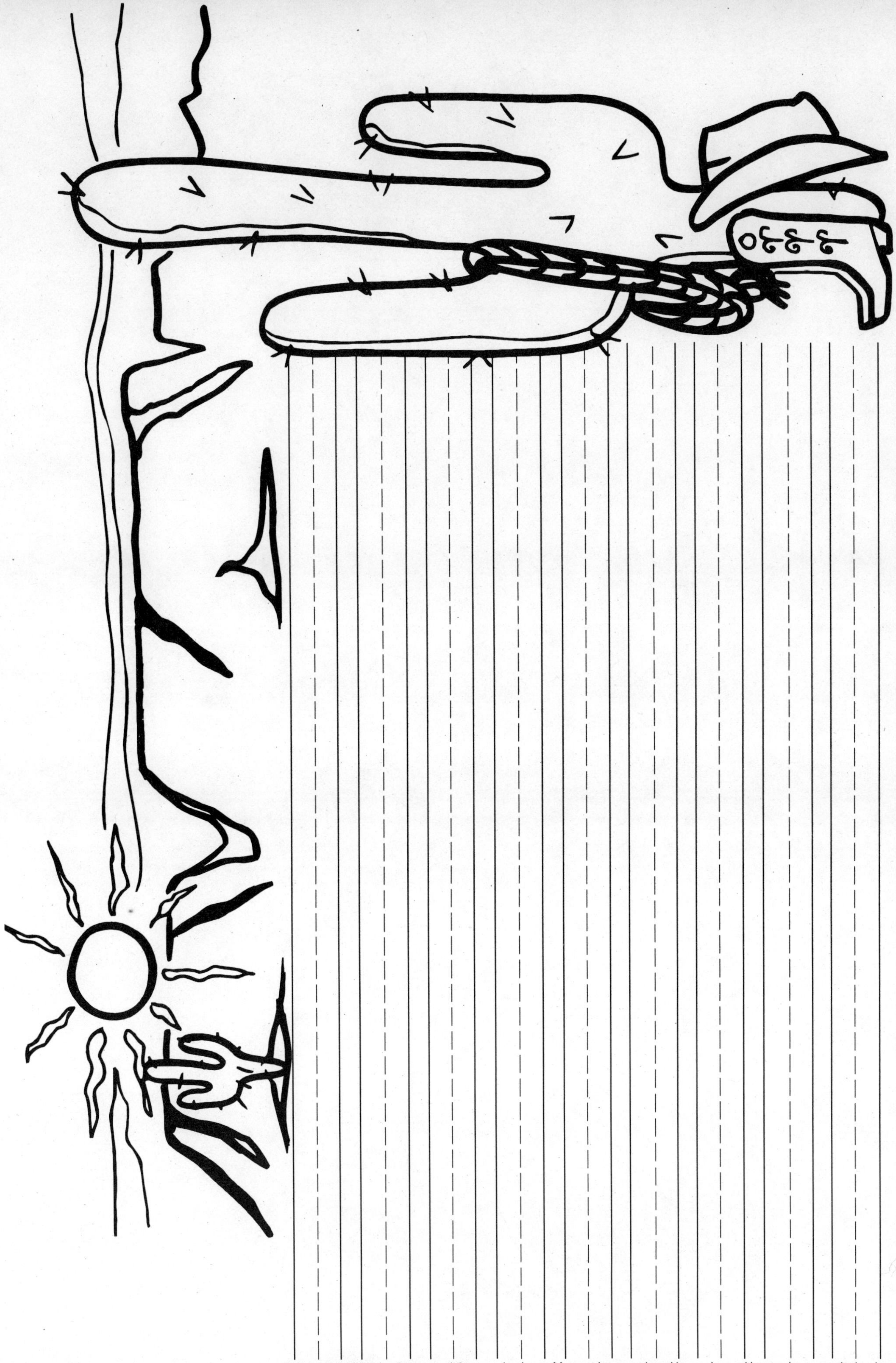

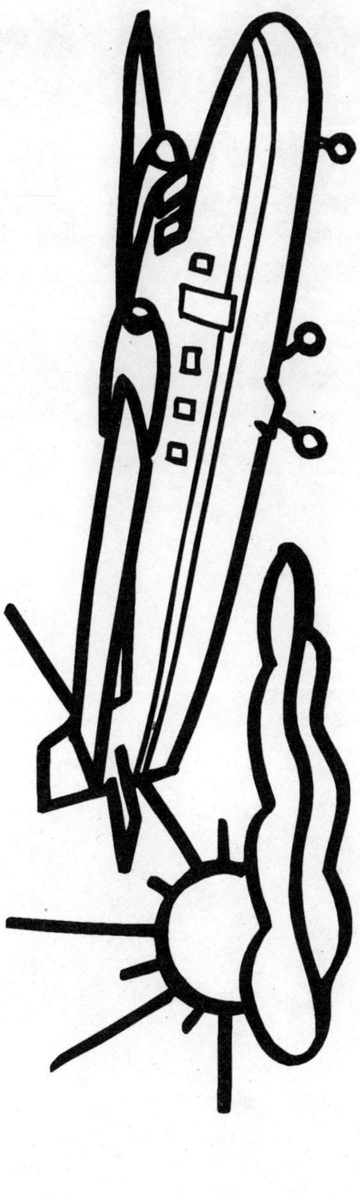

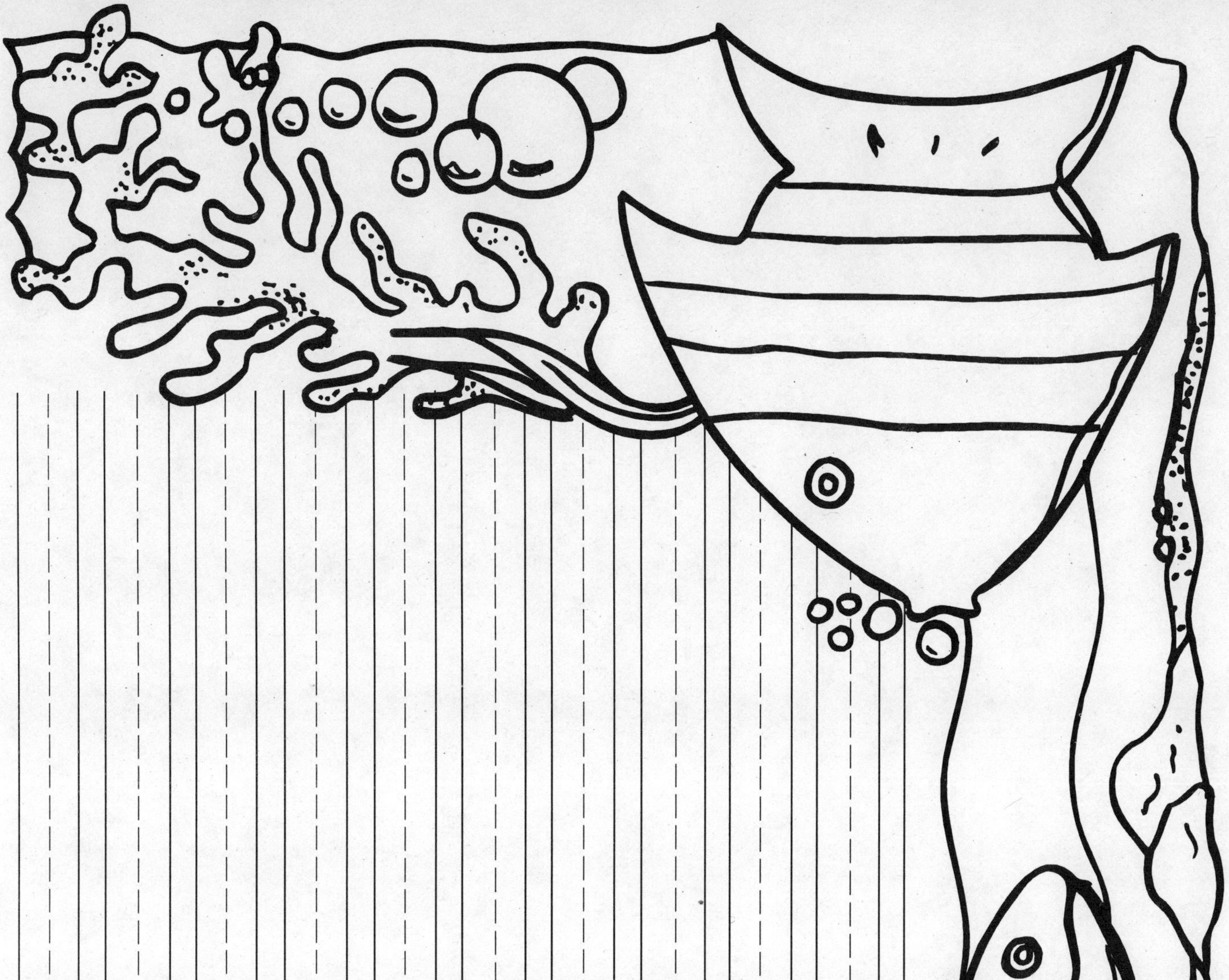

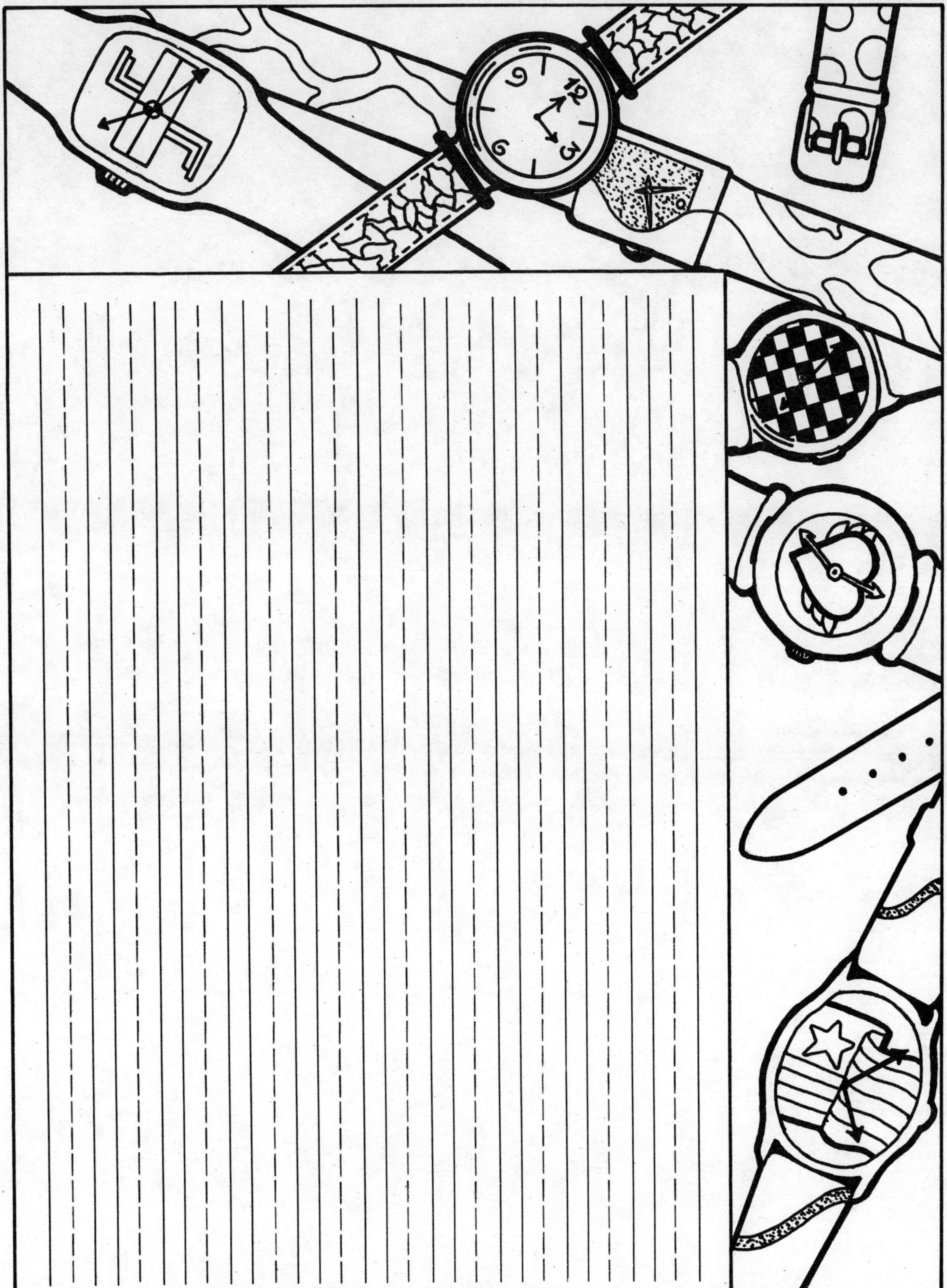

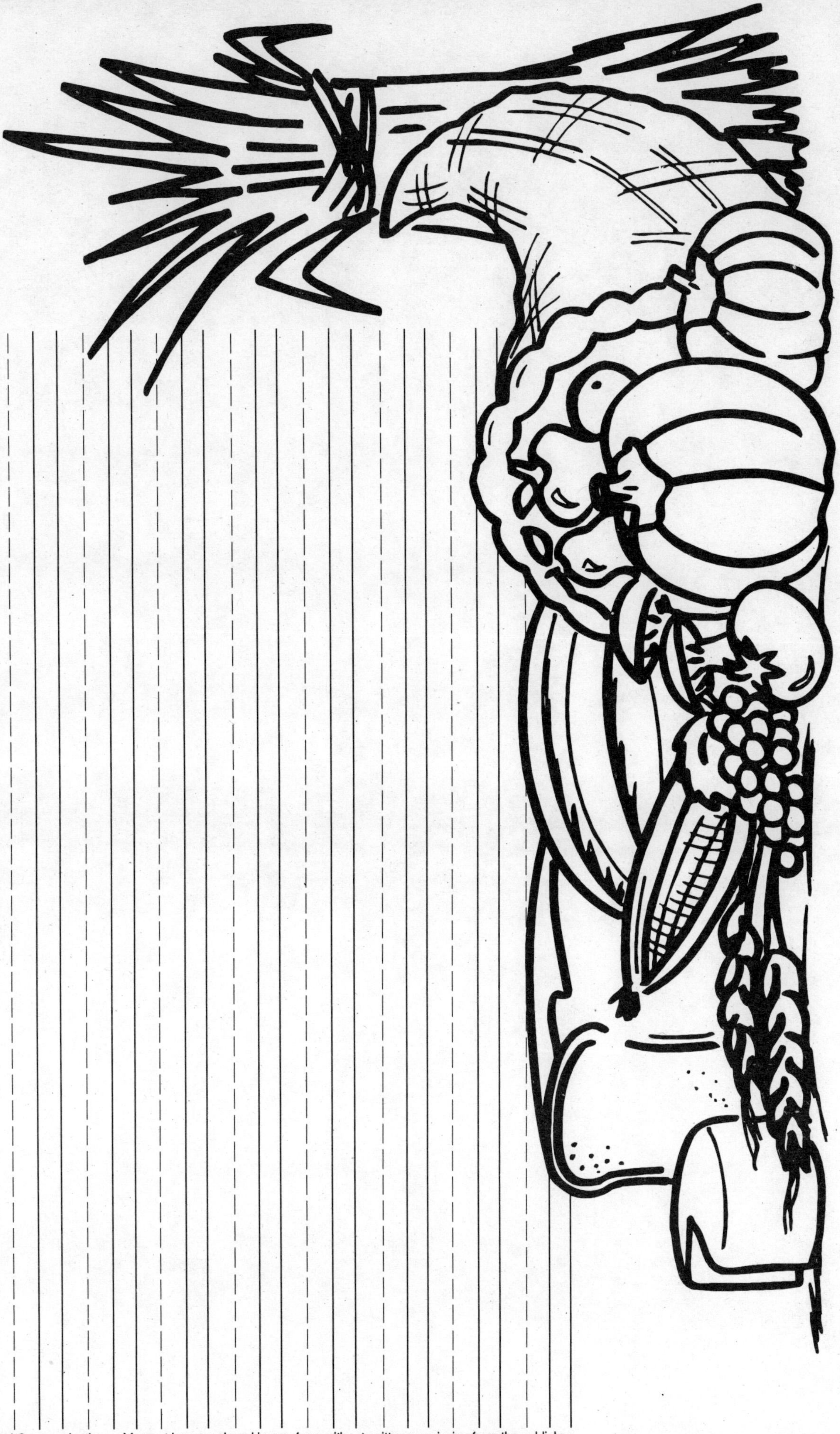

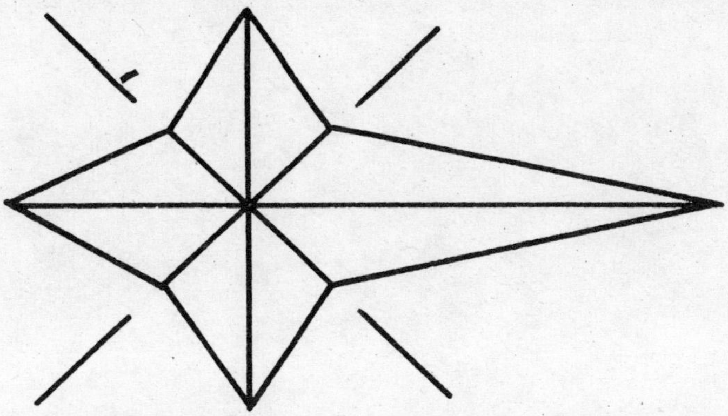

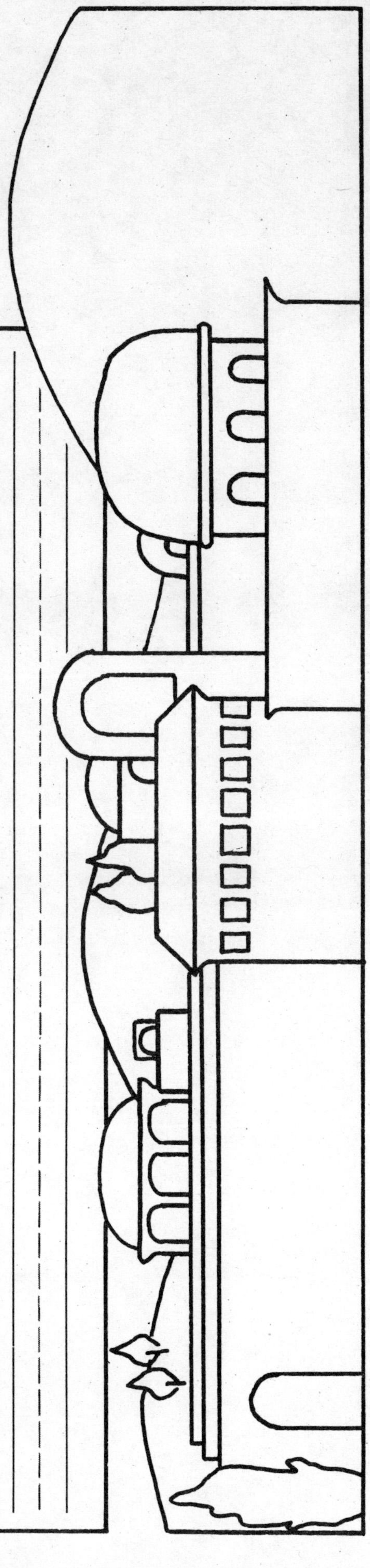

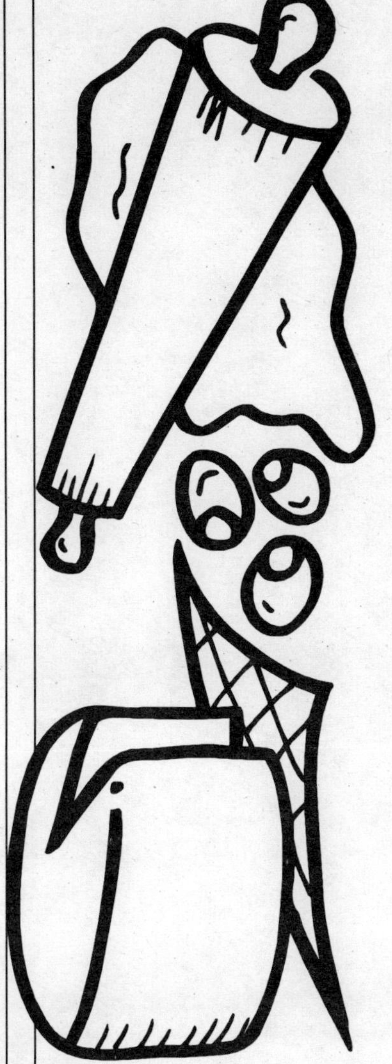

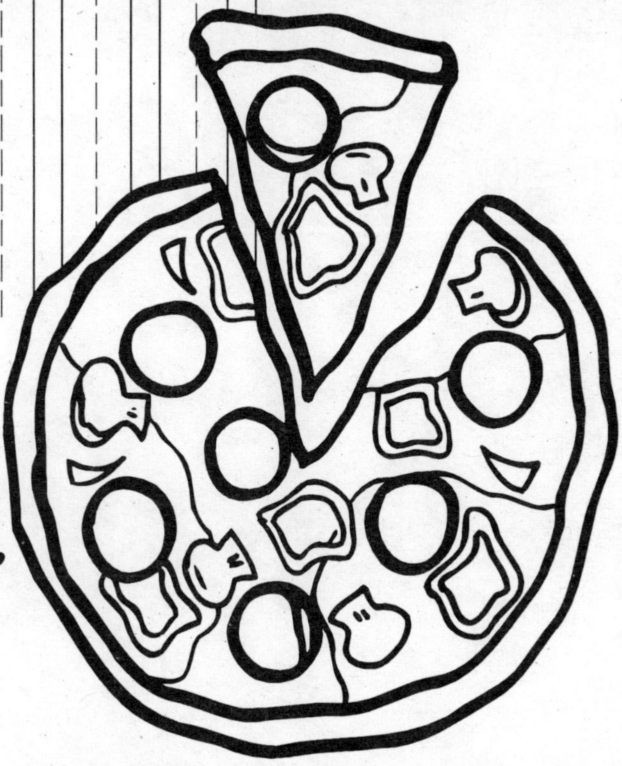

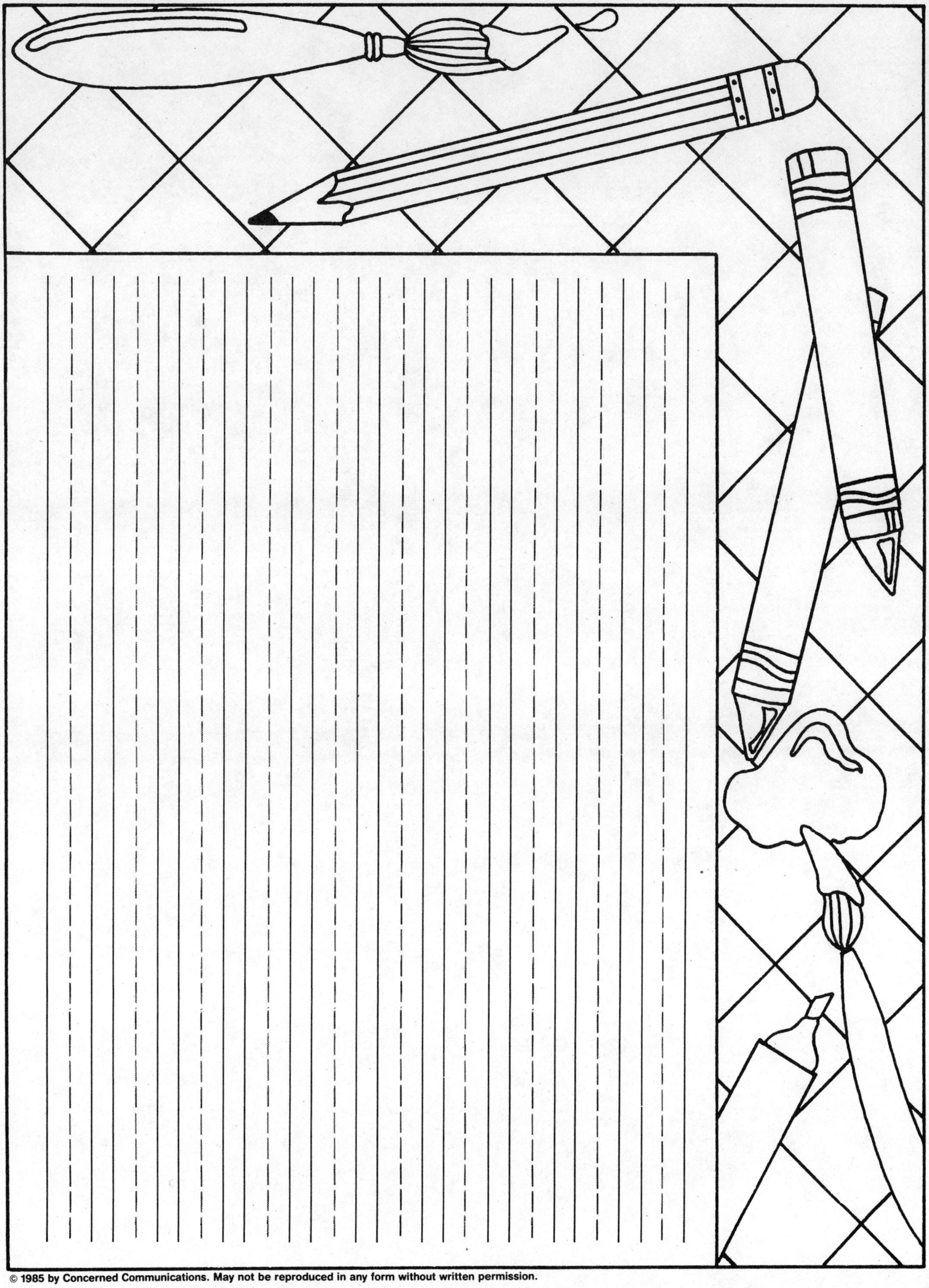

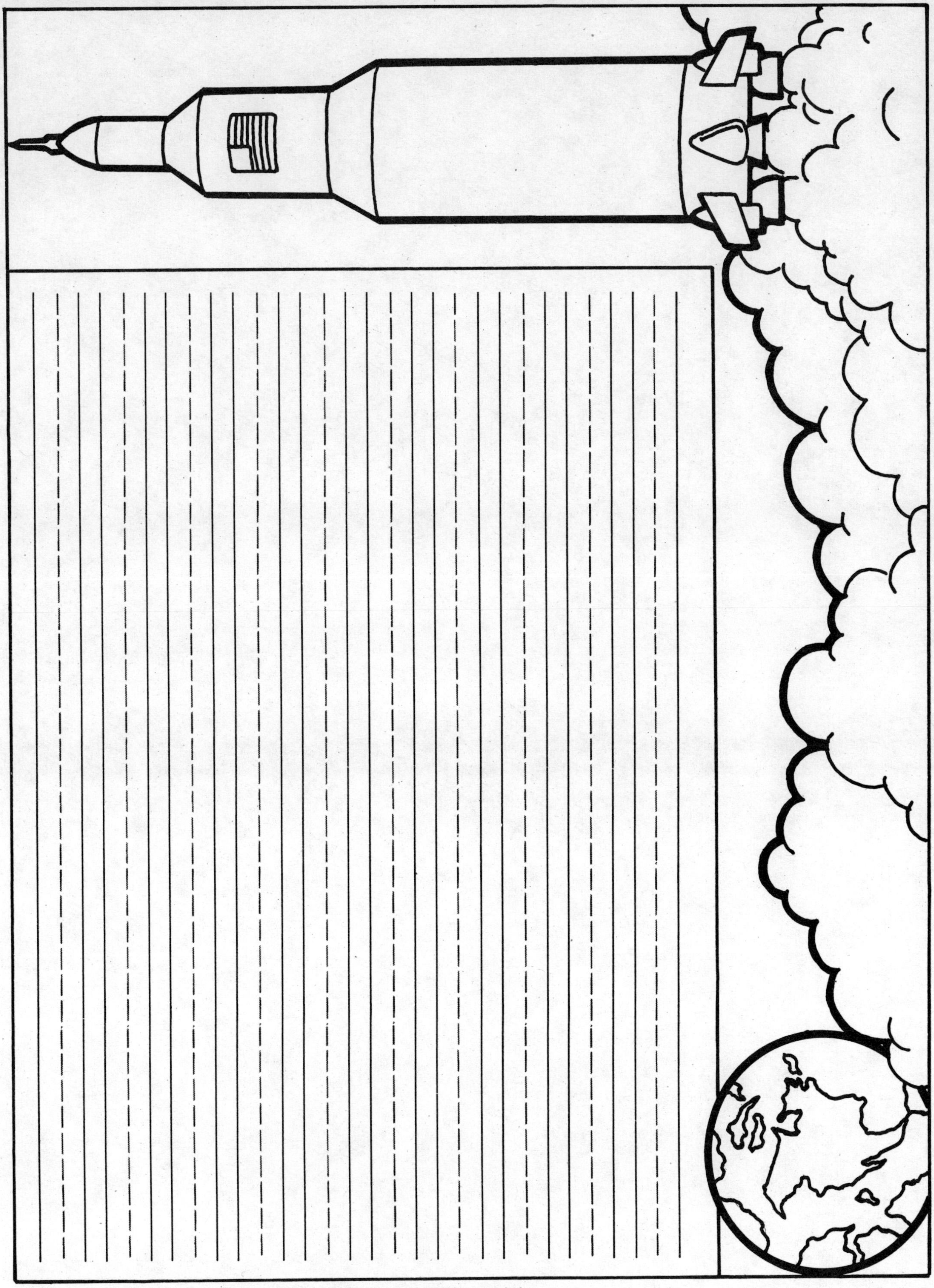

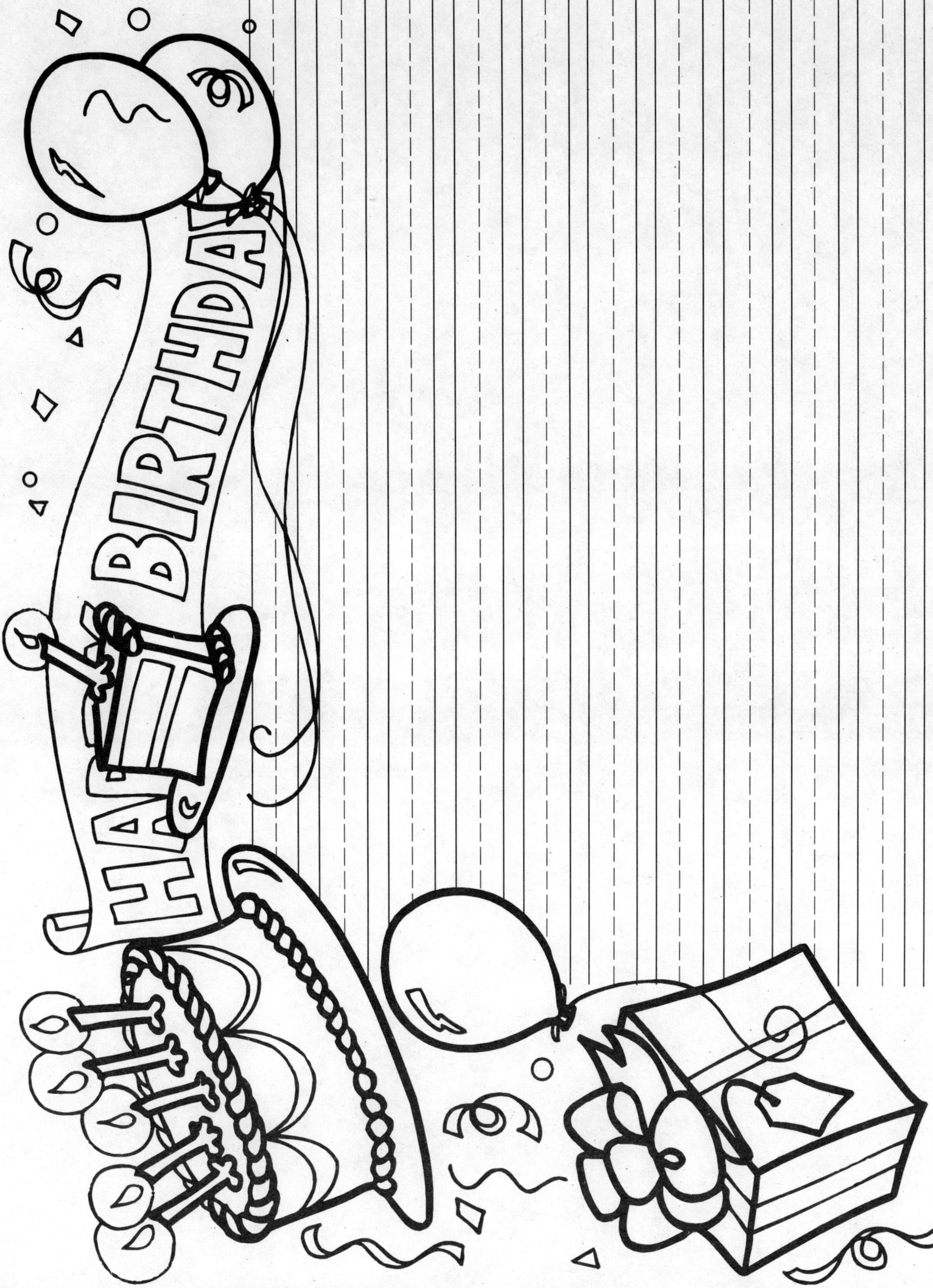
HA
BIRTHDA

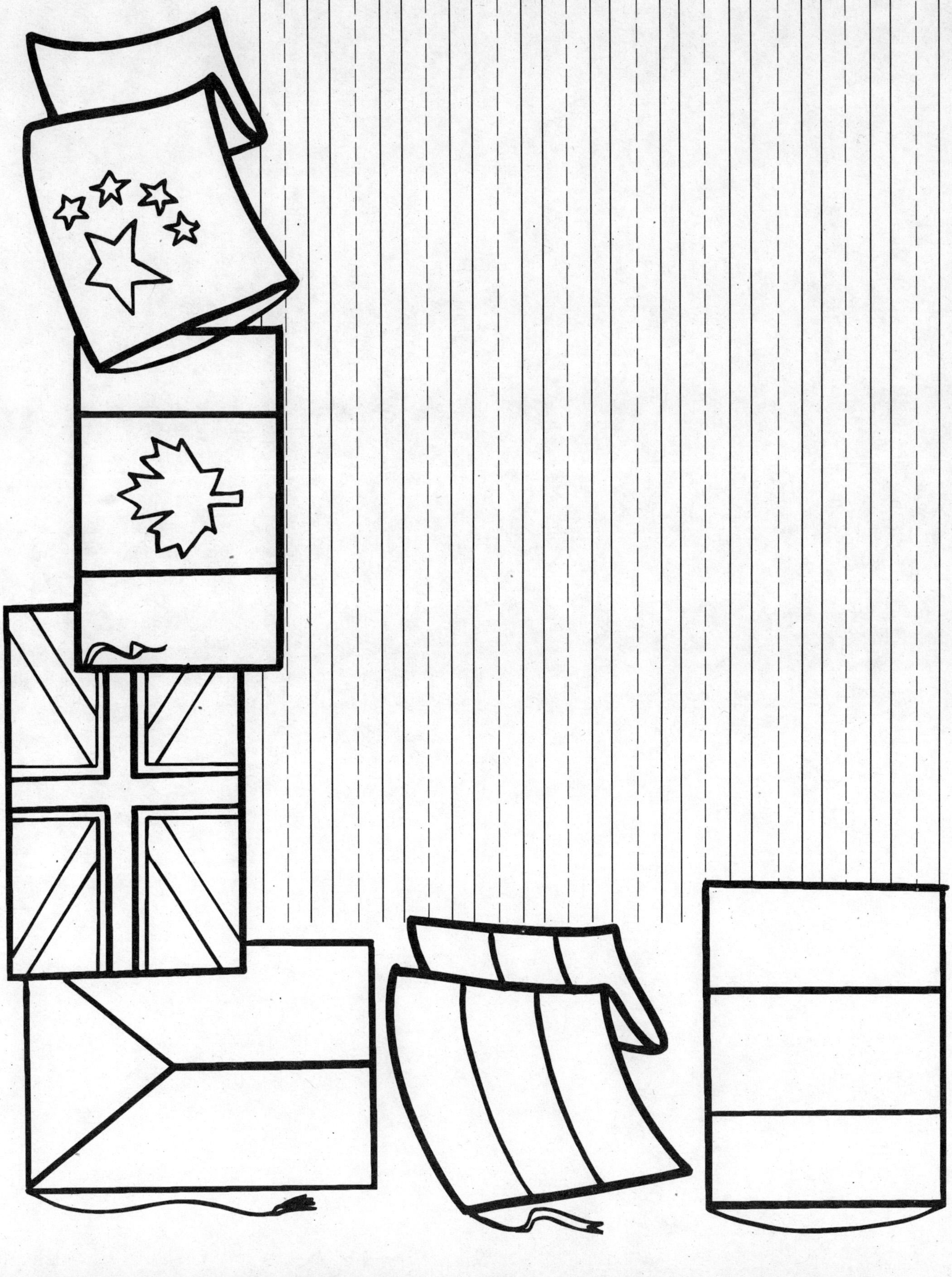

Excellent